Sons of the Revolution

An Account of the Action at Tarrytown on July Fifteenth

1781

Sons of the Revolution

An Account of the Action at Tarrytown on July Fifteenth 1781

ISBN/EAN: 9783337231965

Printed in Europe, USA, Canada, Australia, Japan

Cover: Foto ©ninafisch / pixelio.de

More available books at **www.hansebooks.com**

An ACCOUNT of the ACTION at TARRYTOWN on July Fifteenth, 1781

And of Its Commemoration by the SONS of the REVOLUTION of TARRYTOWN on July Fifteenth, 1899

Printed at The Winthrop Press, New York, M DCCC XCIX

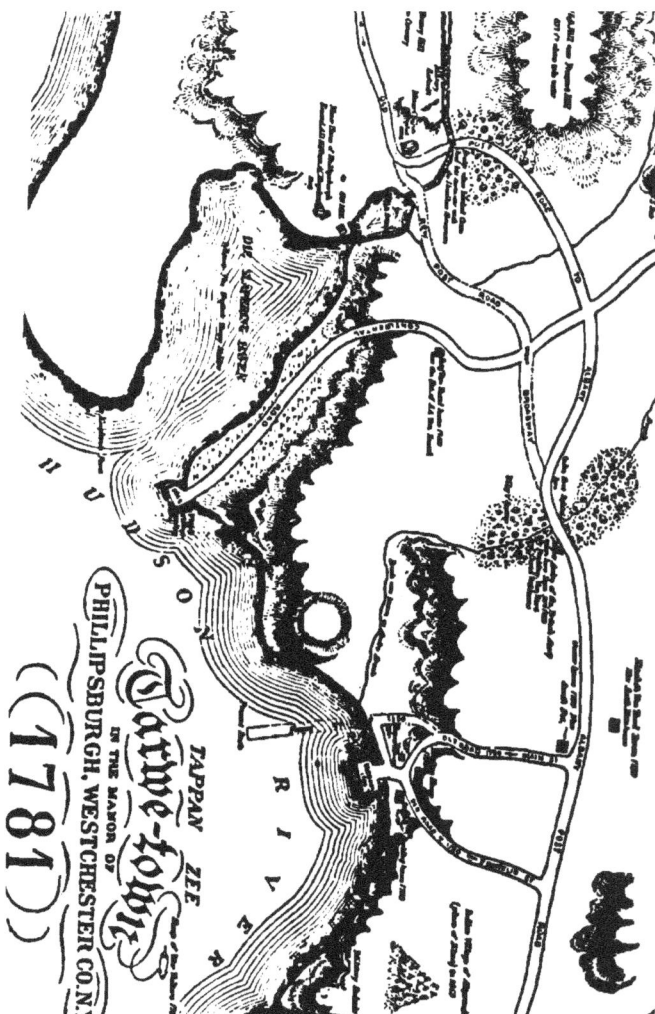

TAPPAN ZEE Tappe-town IN THE MANOR OF PHILLIPSBURGH, WESTCHESTER CO.N.Y. ((1781))

DEDICATION.

This volume contains an accurate history of the Action at Tarrytown, on July 15, 1781, together with an account of the unveiling of the tablet erected to commemorate that event, on July 15, 1899. It thus becomes an important part of the memorial planned by the Sons of the Revolution of Tarrytown in honor of the action and of the men who participated in it, and as such it is gratefully inscribed to those whose generosity made both it and the tablet possible.

RICHARD B. COUTANT, } *Committee*
MARCIUS D. RAYMOND, } *on*
GEORGE C. ANDREWS, } *Publication.*

Tarrytown, N. Y., Aug. 15, 1899.

The Action at Tarrytown

THE ACTION AT TARRYTOWN.

THE HEROISM OF COLONEL ELISHA SHELDON, CAPTAIN GEORGE HURLBUT, CAPTAIN-LIEUTENANT MILES AND LIEUTENANT JOSEPH SHAYLOR.

GREATNESS of reputation does not guarantee a corresponding degree of merit, neither does lack of reputation prove merit to be wanting. Accidents of fortune may bestow honor where it is undeserved, or they may deprive men of honor when it is due. The fame of Paulding and his associates so completely obscures that of all other patriots whose names belong to the history of Tarrytown during the Revolution, that the latter are seldom mentioned in connection with the time or the place. Yet the captors of André are famed not so much on account of what they personally accomplished as because of the importance of the event in which they participated. The merit of their performance did not consist in wisely laid or in bravely executed plans—for their exploit was unpremeditated and they risked neither life nor limb in the prosecution of it—but is to be found in the fact that they were patriotic enough to refuse to release the British spy who had blundered into their hands, when they were tempted to do so by an offer of gold,

The captors were generously rewarded, for, in addition to the honor they received, they were publicly thanked for their fidelity, were pensioned, presented with farms and decorated with medals while they lived. and awarded monuments at public expense when they died. They were justly entitled to the material part of their reward, but the reputation they acquired far exceeded their merit. They unwittingly thwarted a dangerous plot, and were thus made famous by good fortune, while men of greater worth, whom fortune did not favor, lived and died unnoticed and have been forgotten. Among the latter are Colonel Elisha Sheldon and Captain George Hurlbut, of the Second Light Dra. goons; Captain-Lieutenant John Miles, of the Second Continental Artillery, and Lieutenant Joseph Shaylor, of the Fourth Connecticut Infantry, who especially distinguished themselves in the engagement known as " The Action at Tarrytown."

At the date of the action at Tarrytown, July 15, 1781, Washington had given up his plan of a combined attack of the French and American forces on New York, having in contemplation a movement to the south, which three months later resulted in the surrender of Cornwallis and his army at Yorktown. Washington had his headquarters at Dobbs Ferry, and his own and Rochambeau's troops were encamped in the vicinity, their lines extending across the country from the Hudson to the Bronx. The presence of the army at this point was due to the fact that it was necessary to keep up the pretence of an attack on New York to cover the real designs of the commander-in-chief. One month later the troops moved to Kings Ferry, where they crossed the Hudson and began their long march to Virginia. While the army was at Dobbs Ferry large supplies of food and stores were constantly passing down the river by sloop, from West Point and elsewhere, and it was an attempt on the part of the British to destroy certain vessels thus laden that gave rise to the action at Tarrytown. The affair took place in the evening, a short distance from the shore, on a line with what is known as the old Martling-Requa Dock. Not being of sufficient importance to merit mention in works on general history, accounts of it must be sought for in out of the way sources, such as letters, journals and newspapers of the time.

The following account is taken from " Les Français en Amerique pendant la Guerre de l'Independence des Etats-Unis 1777-1783. Par Thomas Balch, Paris 1872. Translation by Rev. Dr. John A. Todd, Scharf's Westchester Co. Vol. 2, p. 230.

" The 15th, at nine o'clock in the evening, the firing of cannon was heard from the direction of Tarrytown, followed by a sharp fusillade. M. de Marquis de Laval immediately caused the drums to be beaten, and the alarm-cannon to be twice discharged. In an instant the army was on foot, but M. de Rochambeau ordered the soldiers to return to camp.

" An hour afterward, Washington asked of him two hundred men, with six cannon and six howitzers, but at the moment in which this artillery should set out they received another countermand.

" The next morning at five o'clock there was a similar alarm, followed by a new demand for two twelve pounders and two howitzers.

" This time G. de Deux Ponts set out in advance for Tarrytown, and Cromot du Bourg, who was in service near M. de Rochambeau, was charged with conducting the artillery. He performed this mission with ardor, for he went under fire for the first time. The cannon arrived at Tarrytown at eleven o'clock. The cause of all these alarms was two English frigates and three schooners, which had ascended the Hudson and endeavored to seize five sailing vessels, laden with flour, which they were transporting from the Jerseys to Tarrytown, for supplying the army. Another ship had already been taken during the night; it contained bread for four days, intended for the French. On account of this loss each soldier was reduced to four ounces of bread. They were given some rice, and besides some meat; they sustained these passing hardship with a gayety and firmness, of which their officers gave them an example.

" Upon the vessel seized by the English was some clothing for the Sheldon Dragoons. The frigates had finally placed their crews in their long boats, in order to effect a landing, and to seize the remaining stores at Tarrytown, but a sergeant of Soissonnais, who guarded that post with twelve men, kept up such a sharp and well-directed fire that the English continued to remain in their boats. A half hour after came the Americans, who had a sergeant lost there and had an officer wounded. Happily in the meantime the four pieces of French artillery arrived; they placed them together in a battery and discharged one hundred shots, which compelled the frigates to retire. They remained in sight during the 17th and 18th. During this time M. de Rochambeau had commanded M. M. de Neuris and de Vertun, officers of artillery, to establish a small battery of two pieces of cannon and two howitzers at Dobbs Ferry, at the narrowest point of the river. The frigates had to pass before this post on the 19th, in order to return to Kings Bridge. They were received with energy. Two shells thrown on board; one of them set it on fire. A French prisoner who was on board, profited by it to escape, but fright soon drove seven of the sailors to throw themselves into the water. Some were drowned, three were taken prisoners and the others regained the frigate upon which the flames had been extinguished."

Dr. Thacher in his "Military Journal" briefly refers to the action as follows :

July 15.—Two of the British frigates and several smaller vessels passed up the North River as far as Tarrytown, in defiance of our cannon, which were continually playing on them. Their object appears to be to seize some of our small vessels which are passing down the river with supplies for our army. One small sloop loaded with bread for the French army has fallen into their hands.

Count William de Deux Ponts, who was with the French allies at Dobbs Ferry, makes the following mention of the action :

On the 15th of July, at half-past ten o'clock in the evening, we heard several reports of cannon and musketry, and a moment after they beat the *générale*. The whole army rushed to arms and was formed in an instant. After having remained in line of battle for half or three quarters of an hour, we received orders to return to our tents. On the morning of the 16th of July I learned that the guns heard yesterday had been fired at Tarrytown, a small place on the banks of the Hudson River, where they have been in the habit of unloading flour, which comes to us from the Jerseys, by two English frigates which wanted to support the attack made by three English schooners with the intention of seizing and burning five small vessels laden with flour. The attack was unsuccessful; indeed they succeeded in setting fire to one of these vessels, but it was put out and the cargo saved.

General Washington, in his journal for 1781, preserved in the library of the Department of State, at Washington, thus notes the details of the encounter:

July 15.—The *Savage*, sloop of war, of 16 guns, the ship *General Washington*, lately taken by the enemy, a ten galley, and two other sma[ll] armed vessels, passed our post at Dobbs Ferry (which was not in a condition to oppose them). At the same time three or four river vessels with 4 eighteen-pounders, stores, etc., had just arrived at Tarrytown, and *with infinite difficulty and by great exertion of Colonel Sheldon, Captain Hurlbut (who got wounded), Captain-Lieutenant Miles of the Artillery, and Lieutenant Shaylor*, were prevented falling into the hands of the enemy as they got aground one hundred yards from the Dock, and were set fire to by the enemy, but extinguished by *the extraordinary activity and spirit of the above gentlemen.*

The only full and satisfactory account of the action is to be found in Moore's " Diary of the American Revolution," where it is copied from the " New Jersey Gazette " of August 8, 1781 :

July 20, 1781.—On Sunday evening, the 15th inst., two sloops of war, two tenders, and one galley, all British, came up the Hudson River with intention, it is supposed, to destroy the stores then moving from West Point to the army. There were at that time two sloops going down the river laden with cannon and powder. As soon as they discovered the enemy they put about and stood in for Tarrytown, where they ran aground. The enemy, having a fair wind and tide, came up the river so fast that it was impossible to march the infantry down in time to unload or protect the stores, as there were no troops at Tarrytown, except a sergeant's guard of French infantry. Colonel Sheldon (whose regiment lay at Dobb's Ferry) immediately marched his mounted dragoons to the place, where he ordered his men to dismount and assist in unloading the stores, which they did with great dispatch. By this time, the enemy having come to anchor off Tarrytown, began a heavy cannonade, under cover of which they sent two gun-boats and four barges to destroy the vessels.

Captain Hurlbut, of the second regiment of light dragoons, was stationed on board of one of these, with twelve men, armed only with pistols and swords. He kept his men concealed until the enemy were alongside, when he gave them a fire, which they returned and killed one of his men. Captain Hurlbut, finding himself surrounded, ordered his men to jump overboard and make for the shore, which they did, he following. The enemy immediately boarded and set fire to the vessels, but were obliged as quickly to retire, owing to the severe fire that was kept up by the dragoons and French guard. Captain Hurlbut, Captain-Lieutenant Miles, Quartermaster Shaylor, and others, jumped into the river and made for the sloop, in order to extinguish the fire, which they did, and saved the vessels. While in the water, Captain Hurlbut received a musket ball through his thigh.

Washington, in the general orders of July 19, 1781, thus refers to Colonel Sheldon and his companions:

" The Commander-in-Chief is exceedingly pleased with the conduct of Major-General Howe for marching with so much alacrity and rapidity to the defense of the stores at Tarrytown and repulsing the enemy from there. He requests General Howe and all the officers and soldiers of the American and French armies who were employed on the occasion to accept this public acknowledgment of their services.

" *The gallant behavior and spirited exertions of Colonel Sheldon and Captain Hurlbut of the Second Regiment of dragoons, Captain-Lieutenant Miles of the Artillery, and Lieutenant Shaylor of the Fourth Connecticut regiment*, previous to the arrival of the troops, in extinguishing the flames of the vessels which had been set on fire by the enemy, and preserving the whole of the ordnance and stores from destruction, *entitles them to the most distinguished notice and applause of their general.*"

As soon as Captain Hurlbut recovered from his wound, he returned to his command, and upon his first appearance before his troops they honored him with a salute. His horse being unused to firearms became unmanageable, and Hurlbut, weak from his long confinement, was thrown violently to the ground. As a consequence, his wound re-opened, and after months of suffering he was sent home to die, the commander-in-chief of the army giving particular orders as to his removal. He survived until the 8th of May, 1783. In 1808 his sister wrote as follows to the Hon. Gideon Granger, Postmaster-General :

Dire necessity induces me, though unknown to you, to trouble you in a matter in which I am deeply interested. I am the widow of Captain John Welsh, who commanded the marines in the unfortunate attack upon Penobscot, in which he lost his life while bravely fighting at the head

of them. The loss of my husband left me in very dis-
agreeable circumstances, which the kindness of a brother
in a measure relieved. This brother was Captain George
Hurlbut, who commanded a company of light horse in
Sheldon's regiment, till in defending a vessel with stores
in the North River he received a wound, under which he
languished till the 8th day of May, 1783, when he expired,
having suffered the most excruciating pain beyond the
power of language to express. This deserving brother
having made a will in my favor and appointed me execu-
trix, I have applied to Congress for the commutation
notes due him, but finding Captain Hurlbut's miserable
life was not continued to the close of the war, they
refused them, though so small a recompense for a life
spent and lost in the service of, I am sorry to say, an
ungrateful country. Should you, sir, think it beneath
your notice to interest yourself for me, I must sit down in
despair. I ask but for twenty or thirty pounds a year to
enable me to pass the evening of my days in peace and
quietness.

Several years prior to the date of this letter, Mrs.
Welsh had written to General and Mrs. Washington
in regard to her claims against the government, and
had received from them the following replies:

FROM MRS. WASHINGTON.

MOUNT VERNON, }
December 8, 1788. }

MADAM :

You may readily conceive that I felt sensible for your
situation, and that were it as much in my power as it is in
my desire I would contribute effectually to your relief.
After having said this, I need only add, that as the
general possesses the same good disposition toward you,

and writes on the subject himself, it is unnecessary for me to say more than that my best wishes attend you, and that I am, madam, your most obedient servant,

M. WASHINGTON.

FROM GENERAL WASHINGTON.

MOUNT VERNON, }
December 8, 1788. }

MADAM :

I received your melancholy letter by the last mail, and could not delay my sympathetic condolence on your unhappy situation. It is, indeed, distressing to me to find that a lady whose husband and brother perished in the service of their country should be reduced to a precarious dependence on others for that support which she might otherwise have received from them. Your affecting case, and others of a similar nature, make me almost weary of living in a world where I can do so little but pity, without having the power to relieve such unmerited misfortunes. If my means were as ample as my wishes, be assured, madam, I am too well persuaded of the hardships of your condition, and *the merit of your brother* not to exert myself effectually for your succor. A private citizen as I am, I know not what I can do (without the appearance of assuming too much upon myself), except to give a certificate of the facts respecting *the brilliant service which your brother performed* at the moment when he met with the wound which occasioned his death, together with a private opinion annexed to it. Of that certificate you may make such use as you shall think proper in application to the Board of Treasury, the Commissioners for settling the accounts of the army, or any other persons to whom the business may appertain. Recommending you most devoutly to that Being who will take care of the widow and the fatherless, even though they should be neglected by an ungrateful country, I remain with ardent wishes for your happiness, madam, your most obedient, humble servant,

GEORGE WASHINGTON.

P. S.—There can be no doubt that, as heir to your brother, you are entitled to that portion of land promised to all officers of his rank who served through the war or died in the service.

The certificate referred to above accompanied the letter, and is as follows :

I do hereby certify to all whom it may concern that Captain George Hurlbut, of the Second Regiment of Light Dragoons, *received a wound in the gallant performance of his duty at Tarrytown* in the summer of 1781, of which, after having languished in the most exquisite pains until the 8th of May, 1783, he expired ; and I do further make known (as my own private opinion), *from the very brave manner* in which he saved a considerable quantity of stores, by swimming on board a vessel and extinguishing the flames that had been kindled by the enemy, amidst a severe fire from their ships (for which he then received my particular thanks in the public orders of the army), as well as from his having survived until after the war was in fact concluded by the signature of the provisional treaty of peace, that the heir or heirs of the said Captain George Hurlbut ought, in point of justice and the reason of the case, to be entitled to the commutation of his half pay, in as full a manner as if he had not died until after the formal disbanding of the army by a reso-lution of Congress. In faith whereof I have here-unto signed my name and affixed my seal this 8th day of December, in the year 1788.

GEORGE WASHINGTON.

General Washington's opinion in regard to the

heroism of Captain George Hurlbut, expressed in
the above letter and certificate, applies equally well
to his companions in danger, and taken in connection with the entry in his journal and his general order relating to them, it confers upon each
of them a distinction which is unique in the annals
of the Revolution. We are compelled to take account of the action, and to admire and respect the
men who made it notable, because Washington set
the seal of his approval upon them in an especial
manner. One cannot read his oft-repeated words of
praise, which we have had set in italics, without
being convinced that Sheldon, Hurlbut, Miles and
Shaylor were heroes in his eyes, and as such we
must also rate and honor them.

The following facts relating to their military services have been compiled from official sources:

ELISHA SHELDON, of Salisbury, Conn., Major Com-
mandant, Battalion of Connecticut Light Horse, June,
1776; Colonel Second Continental Dragoons, December
12, 1776; served to close of war; held right of line in the
advance through Tarrytown on the third of July, 1781;
was a member of the Society of Cincinnati; removed to
Vermont and died there.

GEORGE HURLBUT, of New London, Conn., volunteer
in Lexington Alarm, April, 1775; Sergeant Seventh
Conn., July 8 to December, 1775; Ensign Nineteenth
Continental Infantry, January 1 to December 31, 1776;
Cornet Second Continental Dragoons, April 12, 1777;
Lieutenant, December 25, 1777; Captain, August 1, 1779;
died of wounds received at Tarrytown, May 23, 1783;
buried at New London, Conn.

JOHN MILES, of New Haven, Conn., First Lieutenant Second Continental Artillery, January 1, 1777; Captain-Lieutenant, September 20, 1779; served to June, 1783.

JOSEPH SHAYLOR, of Wallingford, Conn., Volunteer at Lexington Alarm; Ensign of Douglass' Connecticut Regiment, June 20 to December 25, 1776; Second Lieutenant Sixth Connecticut, January 1, 1777; First Lieutenant, November 15, 1778; transferred to Fourth Connecticut, January 1, 1781; served to June 3, 1783; Captain Second U. S. Infantry, March 4, 1791; assigned to Sub-Legion, September 4, 1792; Major Sub-Legion, October 1, 1793; assigned to Second Infantry, November 1, 1796; resigned May 16, 1797; member of the Society of the Cincinnati; died March 4, 1816; was at battle of White Plains.

The foregoing historical data it must be admitted is good and sufficient justification for the erection of the tablet commemorating "The Action at Tarrytown," and so rescuing it from the forgetfulness of oblivion. In fact, the placing of a memento of it had been for some time considered, a fact which accentuated the prompt action that resulted in the placing of a bronze tablet on the walls of the Tarrytown railroad station. This was dedicated with becoming ceremonial on the 15th of July, 1899, the 118th anniversary of the event. So prompt was the response of the patriotic people of this place and vicinity to the call made upon them, and so expeditiously was the design wrought out by the Bonnard Bronze Company, of New York, that but five weeks elapsed from the inception to its completion.

The work was conceived and undertaken by the Sons of the Revolution of Tarrytown, and in carrying it forward to success they were united as to plan and purpose; that everything should be in good taste and in keeping with the traditions and character of this place. The plan and scope were on the lines of a broad and liberal spirit, and the high degree of approbation they received from all interested was sufficient commendation.

The Sons of the Revolution in Tarrytown organized as a Committee of the Whole, with Samuel Requa as Chairman, M. D. Raymond, Secretary, and Isaac Requa, Treasurer, the following members participating in the movement: Dr. R. B. Coutant, Geo. C. Andrews, Frederick G. Le Roy, Wm. C. Strong, D. C. Belknap, James M. Requa, James Bird, Edward Buckhout, Fred. J. Hall, and Joseph E. See.

The following other committees were also appointed:

EXECUTIVE COMMITTEE— Geo. Clinton Andrews, Chairman; M. D. Raymond, Secretary; Jas. M. Requa, D. C. Belknap, Fred. G. Hall, Edward Buckhout.

INVITATION AND RECEPTION COMMITTEE—Samuel Requa, Chairman; W. C. Strong, Secretary; Joseph E. See, F. G. LeRoy, Jas. Bird.

COMMITTEE ON DECORATION OF R. R. STATION AND UNVEILING OF TABLET—F. G. LeRoy, D. C. Belknap, W. C. Strong, Edward Buckhout.

COMMITTEE ON PLATFORM—Jas. Bird.

COMMITTEE ON DECORATION ON LYCEUM HALL— Mrs. A. D. Brink, Jr.

COMMITTEE ON PUBLICATION—Dr. R. B. Coutant, M. D. Raymond, Geo. C. Andrews.

THIS TABLET
ERECTED BY THE SONS OF THE REVOLUTION
AND CITIZENS OF THIS VICINITY ON
JULY 15 1899
COMMEMORATES THE ACTION AT TARRYTOWN
WHICH OCCURRED NEAR THIS SPOT
ON JULY 15, 1781
AND ALSO THE HEROISM OF
COLONEL SHELDON AND CAPTAIN HURLBUT
OF THE SECOND REGIMENT OF DRAGOONS
CAPTAIN — LIEUTENANT MILES
OF THE ARTILLERY
AND LIEUTENANT SHAYLOR
OF THE FOURTH CONNECTICUT REGIMENT
WHO RECEIVED THE PARTICULAR THANKS OF GENERAL WASHINGTON
IN THE PUBLIC ORDERS OF THE ARMY FOR THEIR

The Commemoration by the Sons of the Revolution of The Action at Tarrytown

PROGRAM OF EXERCISES.

The following was the program of the exercises of the day which took place at the R. R. Station, the platform being on the west side, adjoining the Tablet:

Music.

Prayer by the Chaplain,
REV. ALEXANDER HAMILTON.

Music.

Unveiling of Tablet by
D. O. ARCHER.

Music.

Presentation Address by
M. D. RAYMOND.

Music.

Dedication Address by
COL. FREDERICK S. TALLMADGE,
President of the Sons of the Revolution of New York.

Music.

Historical Address by
REV. JOHN KNOX ALLEN, D.D.

Benediction.

The following graphic account of the exercises is copied from the Tarrytown *Argus* of the following Saturday, Aug. 22d, under the heading of "The

Tablet Dedication, a very pleasant and successful affair:"

"Rarely has even the sun of Tarrytown shone on a prettier scene than when on the afternoon of Saturday last it rested upon the standards of the Sons of the Revolution engaged in the act of dedicating the Tablet erected in commemoration of the action which took place here on the 15th of July, 1781.

"Hundreds had gathered at the R. R. Station, and among the invited guests there present were those whose presence added much of honor and dignity to the occasion. There were descendants of President John Adams, Alexander Hamilton, Gov. George Clinton, Lt.-Gov. Pierre Van Cortlandt, of the noted Custis family of Virginia, of Capt.-Lieut. Miles, whose name appeared upon the Tablet; Col. Tatnall Paulding of Philadelphia, son of the late Commodore Hiram Paulding and grandson of John Paulding one of the Captors; Col. F. S. Tallmadge, Pres. of the N. Y. Society of the Sons of the Revolution, whose grandfather Benjamin Tallmadge was a Major in Sheldon's Dragoons, who distinguished themselves in 'The Action at Tarrytown;' Secretary General Montgomery of the National Society, and Secretary Ferris of the New York State Society of the Sons of the Revolution. And there were representatives of the Society of the Cincinnati, of the Colonial Wars, of the Colonial Dames, of the War of 1812, of the Daughters of the Revolution and the Daughters of the American Revolution, and of the Mayflower Society, gathered there on that occasion. Certainly a distinguished assemblage.

And it was in such a presence and amid such surroundings, with the air fairly surcharged with patriotism as the salute was fired and music swelled the breeze, that the exercises proceeded according to program, Captain Samuel Requa of the Tarrytown Sons of the Revolution presiding.

"How appropriate that a great-grandson of Alexander Hamilton should officiate as Chaplain on that occasion. And seated near him on the platform was his venerable father, Gen. Alexander Hamilton, of this place.

"And also how fitting that the Tablet should be unveiled by our highly respected and now oldest inhabitant, ex-President, D. O. Archer, himself a Son of the Revolution through descent from Sergt. John Dean, of historic renown. The unveiling was followed by applause many exclaiming upon the beauty of the Tablet, which has been fittingly characterized as 'a poem in bronze.'"

"The brief presentation address by Mr. Raymond, and then the dedication address by Col. F. S. Tallmadge, the veteran President of the Society of the Sons of the Revolution of the State of New York. It was able, dignified, virile, and patriotic, his presence and address adding greatly to the interest of the occasion.

"The historical address by Rev. Dr. Allen was a noble utterance, and up to the high level of his best efforts.

"A collation at Lyceum Hall followed, to which all the guests were invited. The hall was beautifully decorated with flags and bunting, and from behind a screen of palms, gratuitously furnished from Pierson's conservatory, Prof. Fisher's orchestra furnished the music, which gave an added charm to all. The collation was sumptuous and the service perfect. Nearing its close there was 'a feast of reason and flow of soul,' under the direction of Mr. Geo. C. Andrews as toastmaster, in the way of several patriotic impromptu addresses, which gave added interest to the occasion.

"Ex-Judge Isaac N. Mills, on being called out, made a felicitous address on the men and women of the Revolution.

"Gen. Alexander Hamilton patriotically responded for the Society of Cincinnati.

"Col. Richard H. Greene was called out as a representative of the Mayflower Society, and spoke excellently well upon that theme.

Col. Wm. I. Martin, of the Sons of the Revolution, read an interesting paper on the thrilling times of 1781, including 'The action at Tarrytown.'

"Mrs. Samuel Verplank, of Fishkill, responded for the Colonial Dames—briefly and in excellent taste.

"Col. Heermance, of Yonkers, responded for the Yonkers Historical Society and the Loyal Legion, of which he is a member.

"And so these very interesting and enjoyable exercises of the day came to a happy conclusion."

ADDRESS BY THE REV. DR. JOHN KNOX ALLEN.

One hundred and eighteen years ago to-night, on the evening of July 15, 1781, the events which we recall, and of which we dedicate an enduring memorial at this hour, took place. Since then the shore has encroached upon the river, and it may be that just at this point where now only the voice of a man is heard the guns spoke then, for there are those now living who can remember sailing over this very place where we now stand, where at that time there was a depth of ten feet of water. At any rate it is practically certain that my voice can reach at this moment the spot where cannon thundered, and where the glare of the burning vessels illumined the waters in the darkness.

The facts of history which we commemorate have been fittingly and adequately set forth in a paper which was read by Dr. Richard B. Coutant, before the Tarrytown Historical Society, on the one hundred and ninth anniversary of their occurrence, July 15, 1890, and since published by that Society. I can add nothing to the record of those facts as there delineated, for the paper was evidently the result of research and toil, and a labor of love as well. But it is proper, it is even demanded by this occasion, that I should at least sketch again the story of the events we celebrate.

Tarrytown is not without its place in Revolutionary annals. The records show that it had had prominence as a port of shipment before this date. In September of the previous year one of the great events of the struggle had taken place here in the arrest of the spy, Major John André, and a little less than two weeks before, Washington at the head of the Continental Army, the heroes of Saratoga and Trenton, of Brandywine and Valley Forge, had passed through it in the hope of surprising the enemy at New York, in which hope he was sorely disappointed. At the date of " The Action at Tarrytown," he had surrendered the plan of a combined attack of the French and American forces on that city, and was planning a movement to the south, which he began to execute the next month, and which was crowned with success in the capitulation of Cornwallis at Yorktown in October of that year. His headquarters were at Dobbs Ferry, and his lines extended from the Hudson to the Bronx. While his own and the French troops were at Dobbs Ferry, vessels were constantly bringing stores down the river for the supply of the army. The British becoming aware of this, had at this time sent five vessels up the river to intercept the loaded sloops and destroy their supplies. They successfully passed the post at Dobbs Ferry, and encountered the little fleet with its stores opposite this place.

As soon as the sloops discovered the enemy they endeavored to put into Tarrytown, and in the attempt ran aground. Wind and tide were with the enemy; they came to anchor, and began a heavy cannonade, under cover of which they sent smaller boats to destroy the grounded vessels whose supplies of ordnance and flour were so necessary to the patriot army. It was in the defense and rescue of these that the gallant deeds were performed which are the occasion of our gathering this afternoon.

To Washington's army there belonged a regiment of Dragoons of which Colonel Sheldon was commander, in which Geo. Hurlbut was a Captain, and associated with them in this action were Capt.-Lieut. Miles, of the 2d Continental Artillery, and Lieut. Shaylor, of the 4th Conn., all of whose names appear on this tablet. Before the action began they had been dispatched from Dobbs Ferry, had been ordered to dismount, and were assisting with all haste in unloading the stores.

When the gunboats were sent to set fire to the vessels, Captain Hurlbut with twelve men was upon one of these, which they defended bravely, but finding themselves overpowered jumped into the water and swam for the shore. At least one of the vessels was immediately set on fire. The guns of the Dragoons, and of the French Guard stationed at the place quickly caused those who had boarded it, to retire however. The sight of the burning vessel was too much for the men who had just been driven off, and jumping into the water again they made for the sloop, extinguished the fire, and saved the vessel; but one of them, Capt. Hurlbut, received while in the water a musket ball through the thigh, from which wound he suffered for nearly two years and from which he finally died. Over his grave in his native place of New London, Conn., there is a simple headstone which states that he died in the 28th year of his age in consequence of a wound received in the service of his country. He is worthy of special mention; but of equal courage with him, though they did not offer up so great a sacrifice, were those other young men who accepted an equal risk in behalf of their cause. The field of their action was not a great one, the service they rendered was not in one of the most important engagements of the war, but our hearts would have to be dead to all that is brave and manly if they did not respond to the magnifience of the spirit they displayed.

As that paper to which I referred at the start, and to which I am largely indebted for this outline of facts, truly says, "the captors of André are famed not so much on account of what they personally accomplished as because of the importance of the event in which they participated." They risked nothing, and they were generously rewarded. We would not detract from the honor that is justly theirs, but these young men whose names are here inscribed imperilled their lives, and never until this hour have they received any public recognition, except in the words of Washington. In his General Orders issued four days later he speaks of their "gallant behavior and spirited exertions" in "extinguishing the flames of the vessels which had been set on fire by the enemy, and preserving the whole of the ordnance and stores from destruction," which he says, have entitled them " to the most distinguished notice and applause of their General." Who would not have ventured much to win such a recognition from such a source !

We know that the pages of the history of that time are illuminated by many a similar story of devotion and daring. What they did was of a piece with the strenuous life of that day. And the tradition of courage inaugurated in those significant hours has been well sustained in the generations since. In our Civil War it was proved that we were not degenerate sons of noble ancestors. The descendants of the men who fought at Bunker Hill and White Plains, at Trenton and Yorktown, endured hardness through four dreadful years, and whether it were in the weariness of the camp or the shock of battle, were never found wanting. We salute the remnant who are still with us, and with tender feelings we recall the host whose dust is mingled with the soil of many a hard-fought battle-field, which is buried in many a swamp and by the side of many a Southern river, or which was brought back and laid with their kin to sleep until the hour of the reveille. The war for independence was nobly followed by the war for national unity and the freedom of the oppressed. And that again by our recent war in behalf of humanity, when a spirit like that of Continental heroes, like that of the men of '61 animated the hearts of our young men, when Dewey's loud knock was heard on a Sunday morning at the gates of the East when the thunder of his guns woke up the sleepy Orient and was heard around the world, and announced the advent of a new era in the story of mankind. The same courage which we applaud in these men of the past was exhibited by those who pushed through Cuban jungles under a tropic sun, who fought their way up San Juan Hill, or who in camp encountered enemies more to be dreaded than Spanish soldiers, enemies which lurked in the air and which they had never enlisted to fight. Kindred in spirit, but let us say not nobler than that of the men who swam out that night more than a hundred years ago to extinguish the flames that were burning up the precious supplies, was he who, with his little company of seven men, took the vessel devoted to destruction, into the channel of the harbor of Santiago, under the dying moon on another summer night,

" Into the jaws of death,
Into the mouth of hell,"

while from the forts on either hand they were " stormed at with shot and shell." Just as brave were these modern heroes, but no braver than this little company who performed a deed almost unheralded by history.

And while our ears are deafened by the roar of these more recent conflicts, let us not forget that earliest struggle of all, the sound of which comes to us so faintly across the far reaches of a century. If it had not been for those patient, long-suffering men of the past with their indomitable courage ; if it had not been for the poorly disciplined, poorly-fed, poorly-clothed soldiers of that distant day in whose hearts there burned the unquenchable love of liberty; if it had not been for Sheldon and Hurlbut and thousands like them, there would have been no nation for the men of '61 to fight for; no later generation schooled and indoctrinated in the love of brotherman and such an intense hatred of oppression as should lead them instinctively to feel for the sword at the sight of wrongs which, while they were visited upon a people alien in race, were yet suffered by a people who were bound to them by the ties of a common humanity.

It is such deeds as those which we commemorate that consecrate the soil of a land, which increasingly make the planet itself a significant and sacred thing. Just a raw ball of earth it was at the start, with no history, no associations clustering about any spot, but now its surface all haunted by the memory of human experiences, of splendid deeds, of magnificent passages in the story of mankind. The record of what man has done is involved with innumerable places, and they are invested with a fadeless interest. This is what gives travel in older lands than ours such a peculiar charm to the student of history and the man of imagination. "You have no ruins," says Ruskin to us, pityingly, and we have to confess that if you except the human ones, we have few. We know well know what he means; this country is so bare of associations; we can point to no castles in which is incorporated the story of centuries, in which "the stone cries out of the wall, and the beam out of the timber answers it," concerning notable scenes which they have witnessed; in whose decay the passing of a phase of human life is registered. We travel in these lands and there is no bay or headland, no city nor river but that is voiceful concerning an eventful and impressive past. To them belong the places with which is forever entwined the memory of the most sacred facts in the story of man on the earth; to them belong a Bethlehem and a Calvary.

In the eyes of many it is these things which give value to a land, which hallow its shores and mountains. It is the misfortune of our newness that we have as yet comparatively few spots about which such associations hover. But we are gaining them; they are multiplying.

We can point visitors to the rock on which pilgrim feet were set, "the doorstep of a continent," which those stern and rugged men were invading in the name of God and righteousness. We can take men to the Hall which was the true "cradle of liberty," and then conduct them to battle-fields where its infant face was baptized with blood. We can point to the spot where a historical instrument was signed, and then lead them to another where the

martyrs of liberty made good the words of that instrument. We can indicate the place where a
great man entered into life, and whether his tomb
be that stately one yonder on the banks of the
river, or that modest one yonder in the churchyard ;
we feel that these things lend to our land an in-
effaceable charm. So our gray rocks are becoming
eloquent with association, and the waters along our
shores, in which the caravels of Columbus dropped
anchor, above which the Mayflower furled her sails
after her eventful voyage, over which have echoed
the guns of our battleships, are " vocal with heroic
speech." " On this spot," are the appropriate words
with which the inscription on that monument along
the street yonder begins. Thither pilgrim feet come,
upon it the eyes of men linger, and tarrying there
the soul of the reader, as his imagination constructs
anew the events of that fateful morning, is stirred
within him.

We live in one of the most beautiful regions on
the face of the earth, and we cannot lift our eyes
without beholding on every hand the evidences of
surpassing wealth and unexampled material prosperity, but anointed souls will not see in these things
the principal charm of the region ; rather will they
linger in the contemplation of that old church, a
" little gospel parable in gray," so intimately con-
nected with the profoundest interests that belong to
the life of man. They will turn to that monument
on Battle Hill which bears deeply chiseled into its

substance the names of the honored dead, a trust which we hope it will keep until the "leaves of the Judgment Book unfold." They will linger for a while at the place where simple yeomen "baffled the arts of a spy and the plots of a traitor." They will revert in thought to that little library at the south of us, where in quiet and seclusion a rarely gifted man wrote words that have illuminated the minds of a multitude of men. We are called materialistic as a people; men speak of our greed, our inordinate love of money, and we must confess that the indictment has a good deal of truth in it. The fault, however, is not peculiarly American; we share it with our critics. Yet while we confess to the impeachment, we stand here this afternoon under the eaves of this building, and we leave securely fastened to the walls which belong to one of the greatest, wealthiest corporations in the land, this tablet, reared to commemorate a noble, brave, patriotic deed, and in it we herald to the incoming and outgoing traveler two things, one the spirit in which the institutions of this country were conceived, and the other that we do not forget to honor that spirit, that there are some things we cherish besides money, that in the midst of abounding worldly prosperity we are not wholly unmindful of the things that belong to the higher nature.

There are various reasons why we set up such a tablet as that which we unveiled to-day. We do it to discharge an obligation. We do it that the best things in human life may not be lost in oblivion, and such a memorial will serve to fire the hearts of those who are to come after us, and lead them to emulate the noble deeds of those who preceded them. The story of generous acts, whether told on the printed page, or in the sculptured form of statesman or hero or philanthropist, or in enduring bronze at the place where they were done, reminds others that they may make their lives sublime. The boy has them held up to him, and his heart leaps and his blood tingles, and he longs for the hour of manhood to come when he may go out on the world's broad fields of battle, and imitate such deeds. It is affirmed that the decks of English naval ships are recruited from the story of the English naval hero, Nelson. Brave young hearts read the story of the hero of Trafalgar; and passing his magnificent monument in the square in London they learn that that is the kind of life which men delight to honor, and rising above the noisy broadsides of his fleets as they hear them in imagination, above the roar of seas crimsoned by the blood of those who freely offered up their lives, out of the smoke of conflict comes the voice of the man who commands their lives. Though dead he speaks, their eager hearts respond, and from quiet homes all over the wide-spread land they present themselves prepared for the hardships of service, ready to tread the decks slimy with blood, anxious to show themselves one in spirit with the man who sums up for them in himself all that is manly and admirable.

That is one reason why we put up the statues of great men in parks and squares and galleries. It satisfies our hearts to honor them, and then also we know that the mute and marble lips will summon others to tread the paths which these men trod. Said one of the old Greek conquerors who had travelled in his boyhood over the battlefields where Miltiades had won victories and had set up monuments to commemorate them. " These trophies of Miltiades will not let one sleep." They fired his brain, they stimulated his blood, they nerved his hand, and when in later years you came to account for his own masterful deeds, you had to go back to his boyhood's days and the sight of those silent mementoes of the victories of another. We trust that such a tablet as this which we affix to these walls, will never allow our youth to sleep. May the sight of it forbid their ever falling into any lethargy of indifference to what is great and noble; may it rouse them to a sense of what is worthy and beautiful in existence ; may it impress them with the thought that there is something better in life than comfort and worldly goods; may it illustrate the glory of the spirit that stops not to reckon the cost, though it be life itself, in behalf of a splendid cause, and if ever the hour of emergency arises in the land they love, may it lead them to emulate the courage and patriotism which these men exhibited.

When, after the darkness has fallen on this July night, you look from your homes down upon the river, let your imaginations travel back to that corresponding July night, in 1781, that Sunday night, and let them create for you the scene of action as it was, with only a hamlet of a few hundred souls along the water, and with no village with its constellation of lights on the opposite shore. Think of the darkness brooding over all, and the silence suddenly broken by cries of consternation and the booming of cannon, while the river just where we now stand was illuminated by the glare of burning vessels ; then recall these four men and the others who flung themselves into the water and swam out to the imperilled ships and extinguished the flames at risk of life and limb, and as you sit in the midst of peace and plenty, do not fail in admiration of these and others like them who purchased for you the inheritance you enjoy.

www.ingramcontent.com/pod-product-compliance
Lightning Source LLC
Chambersburg PA
CBHW021441090426
42739CB00009B/1585